MONSTERS

VAMPIRES

BY RAYMOND H. MILLER

KIDHAVEN PRESS
An imprint of Thomson Gale, a part of The Thomson Corporation

THOMSON
GALE

Detroit • New York • San Francisco • San Diego • New Haven, Conn.
Waterville, Maine • London • Munich

THOMSON

★ ™

GALE

LIBRARY OF CONGRESS CATALOGING-IN-PUBLICATION DATA

Miller, Raymond H., 1967–
   Vampires / by Raymond H. Miller.
      p. cm. — (Monsters)
   Includes bibliographical references and index.
   ISBN 0-7377-2619-9 (hardcover : alk. paper)
   1. Vampires—Juvenile literature. I. Title. II. Monsters series (KidHaven Press)
   GR830.V3M55 2005
   398'.45—dc22
                                                      2004012545

Printed in the United States of America

CONTENTS

CHAPTER 1

THE VAMPIRE STRIKES!

"I am Dracula. I bid you welcome."[1] With those seemingly innocent words, people watching the 1931 movie *Dracula* were invited into the dark and sinister world of the vampire. For many, it was their first glimpse of this terrifying monster. The evil Count Dracula's skin was ghostly white, and his eyes were dark and menacing. He lurked in the shadows of his creepy castle in the mountains of Transylvania. Most frightening of all was his desire to drink the blood of others. The image portrayed by Hollywood made a lasting impression. For the rest of the twentieth century, *Dracula* defined the look and nature of a vampire in the minds of most people.

Dracula emerges from the shadows of his Transylvania castle in the 1931 movie Dracula.

Although *Dracula* made the vampire famous, this fascinating monster has been found in countless stories of many cultures and time periods. However, ancient vampires were much different from the modern, popular version. One of the earliest-known bloodsucking

In this illustration, a bloodsucking strige *holds its victim in place as it feeds.*

creatures is the *strige,* a **mythological** vampire-witch from ancient Greece. The *strige* had the head of a man and the body of a bird. This creature flew around at night snatching children from their cradles and drinking their blood. A similar creature is found in ancient Malaysian folklore. According to legend, the *langsuyar* was a beautiful woman who turned into a demonlike vampire after learning her baby was born dead. She flew down from the trees at night and preyed upon the children of the village.

CREATURES OF THE NIGHT

In the early 1700s, other stories about vampires began to emerge in central and eastern Europe. These accounts came at a time when most people had little understanding of science and the natural world surrounding them. When they experienced something they could not understand or explain, such as the plague, they turned to superstition for answers. Many people believed the bad things that happened in the world were caused by supernatural beings that wanted to harm the living. This is how many vampire stories in Europe were started. The tales nearly always described dead relatives or friends who "issue forth from their graves in the night, attack people sleeping quietly in their beds, suck out all their blood from their bodies and destroy them,"[2] writes vampire expert Montague Summers. Summers wrote many articles about supernatural topics and collected oral and written stories of vampire sightings as part of his research for a book about vampires.

The Vampire Strikes!

Not all descriptions of vampires and vampire attacks are the same, but many details are surprisingly similar. From these descriptions, a haunting picture of vampires emerges. For example, vampires are often described as having bloated bodies, hairy palms, red lips, red eyes, and long, razor-sharp teeth. In many accounts, vampires are seen wearing ragged burial cloths. And, while most vampires described in eyewitness stories are male, some are female and some are children.

In most cases, vampires are described as dwelling in a world between life and death. This is why they are called the **undead**. Vampires, Summers writes, are "neither dead nor alive; but living in death."[3]

During the day, the vampire remains in a coma-like sleep, sometimes underground and sometimes in a coffin. At night it rises from the grave and searches the land for possible victims. One author suggests a vampire is **nocturnal** because the hours between dusk and dawn are "when evil is exalted and the powers of darkness are most active."[4] Arnold Paole and Peter Plogojowitz, two men who were accused of being vampires in the eighteenth century, prowled their villages and attacked people only at night.

A Bloodthirsty Being

In all stories, whether folktales or eyewitness accounts, vampires always thirst for blood. A vam-

A vampire waits in the shadows for its next victim in this scene from the 1979 movie Nosferatu.

pire will drink the blood of an animal when necessary, but always prefers human blood. This is one of the most terrifying characteristics of a vampire. The vampire drinks blood to acquire the victim's energy. Without regular feedings, a vampire will grow weak and eventually die.

The Vampire Strikes!

The desire for the life-giving energy of blood is very strong in some people. "Blood has always been held to possess supernatural and mystical qualities," one researcher writes. Long ago, people probably thought that to "receive it, through drinking or magical infusions, can restore lost power, heal mortal wounds, and grant eternal life."[5] Historians believe this is the reason Elizabeth Bathory, a Hungarian noblewoman born in 1560, desired the blood of others. She tortured and killed more than six hundred young women and girls in hopes that their blood would restore her lost youth. She bathed in and drank their blood, believing it would make her skin smoother and younger looking. While Bathory was not undead, she has been called a living vampire.

Supernatural Powers

Before a vampire can satisfy its need for blood, it must first find a victim. In most instances, victims are easily overpowered. Stories of vampire attacks describe vampires as having great physical strength as well as supernatural powers. These powers are believed to develop and become stronger with age. Some vampires have the ability to use mind control to put a person under their spell.

The vampire's most amazing supernatural power is its ability to **shape-shift**. Vampires are said to be able to magically transform into bats, dogs, wolves, and even fog or mist. They may change shape to avoid capture or to pursue a victim.

Whether the victim is brought under control by force, spell, or illusion, a vampire holds the person close and slowly sinks two long fangs into his or her neck to begin feeding. According to legend, when the fluid in the vampire's mouth enters the victim's bloodstream, it has a powerful, transforming effect. The victim falls into a trance. If the person is not treated immediately, the bite may cause the victim to join the world of the undead. That person will then rise from the grave at night to go out in search of blood.

In this nineteenth-century painting, a priest prays to drive off a vampire in the form of a bat (close-up, inset).

AVOIDING ATTACK

Just as the vampire's personality has taken shape over time, so have the many methods of protection. Through the ages, many different items and techniques have been suggested for protection against vampires. One common method during the sixteenth and seventeenth centuries was hanging garlic by a door or window or wearing a string of it around one's neck. Vampire experts believe the strong scent of garlic is offensive to vampires and will keep them from attacking. Christian symbols, such as the crucifix and holy water, were also thought to be extremely offensive to vampires and have long been used to drive them away.

Some stories even suggested that scattering seeds near a vampire offered protection. Most vampires of folklore were obsessed with cleanliness and could not pass the seeds without stopping to count every one. This gave a potential victim time to escape.

According to most stories, the only real protection against a vampire was to destroy it. Centuries ago, people believed they could destroy a vampire by cutting off its head or burning its body. They also relied on **vampire hunters**. The vampire hunter entered a graveyard at night armed with a gun loaded with a silver bullet. Shooting a vampire with this special bullet was thought to be a sure way to kill it.

Another sure way to kill a vampire was to drive a wooden stake through its heart. This well-known

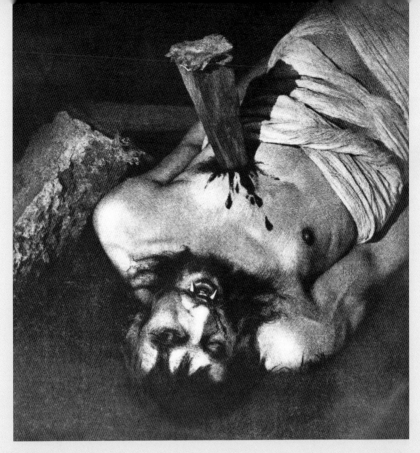

In this engraving, a wooden stake driven through a vampire's heart kills the monster.

method of slaying a vampire dates back centuries. In 1826, for example, a Serbian monk described a scene in which townspeople dug up a suspected vampire and "ran him through with a hawthorn stake."[6]

While most vampire stories are rooted in folklore, there have been people in history who thought they were vampires. At times, they even acted like vampires. Other people have claimed to be the victim of a vampire attack. Often these victims gave convincing details that led others to wonder if vampires really existed.

The Vampire Strikes!

CHAPTER 2

DO VAMPIRES EXIST?

Arnold Paole was the subject of a famous eighteenth-century vampire scare. A former soldier, Paole lived in the Serbian town of Medvegia. He was a hardworking farmer who was known for being honest and good-natured. In 1727, when Paole was in his early twenties, people began noticing a change in him. Those who saw him said he appeared to be troubled. Paole soon confessed that a vampire had bitten him when he was serving in the army. He claimed to have followed the vampire back to its grave and killed it. In an effort to remove the curse, he ate some of the dirt at the grave and tasted the vampire's blood. Even after taking these precautions, he was still convinced he would

14

Vampires are believed to rise from their graves at night to prey on human victims.

turn into a vampire. A week after his confession, he died in an accident and was buried immediately.

Within a month of his burial, people reported seeing visions of Paole. Four people who claimed to have seen him died a short time later. Panic spread through the village. Forty days after Paole's death, community leaders and two military surgeons opened his grave. They expected to find nothing unusual, and they hoped this would calm fears in the village.

Instead they were alarmed by Paole's appearance. His body showed little sign of decay, and he appeared to have fresh blood around his mouth. The corpse also appeared to have newly grown fingernails. As a precaution, they drove a stake into his chest. When they did this, they reported, a loud groan arose from the corpse. Convinced he was a vampire, they burned his body to prevent him from returning from the grave again.

PETER PLOGOJOWITZ

Around the same time as the Paole case, another famous vampire case occurred in a part of Serbia that is now in Hungary. The vampire scare involving Peter Plogojowitz occurred in 1728. Three days after Plogojowitz's death at the age of sixty-two, he reportedly shocked his family by returning to his house. He asked his son for food, which he received and ate, and then left. Two nights later he again returned looking for food but was turned away. The son was found dead the next day.

A winged vampire lands on the head of a sleeping victim in this twentieth-century illustration.

Several days later, some of the villagers fell ill with exhaustion. They were all diagnosed with a large loss of blood. They began having nightmares that Plogojowitz was attacking them in their sleep. The next week, nine of the people died from the mysterious illness. Fears of **vampirism** gripped the village.

A military commander was brought in to investigate the case. He immediately ordered the graves of Plogojowitz and his supposed victims dug up and opened. All of the dead bodies appeared normal except Plogojowitz's. His corpse appeared to be in a trance. His eyes were wide open, and he was said to be breathing faintly. Most frightening was the fresh blood smeared around his mouth. The commander quickly ruled Plogojowitz a vampire and had someone drive a stake through his chest. To complete the destruction, the villagers burned his corpse. Afterward, there were no further reports of Plogojowitz terrorizing the community.

VAMPIRE OF CROGLIN GRANGE

Nearly 150 years later, author August Hare investigated a story about a vampire encounter in England. According to Hare's telling, a woman and her two

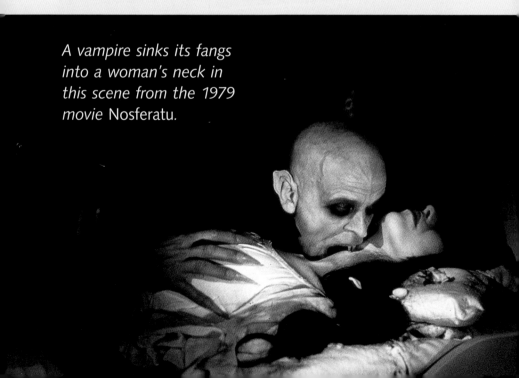

A vampire sinks its fangs into a woman's neck in this scene from the 1979 movie Nosferatu.

brothers were spending the summer of 1875 at Croglin Grange, a house in Cumberland, England. Late one night, the woman was startled by two bright points of light shining through her bedroom window. She soon realized the points were not lights, but the eyes of a dark, humanlike creature. The eyes moved closer and closer until they were just outside her window. The monster then entered the bedroom through the window and attacked the woman. The brothers heard their sister's screams and ran to help. One tended to his fallen sister, while the other chased the creature into the woods. It escaped by leaping over a wall, then ran through a church graveyard.

The woman had two small puncture marks on her neck. She was shaken by the attack, but the wounds eventually healed. On her doctor's orders, the woman and her brothers went to Switzerland for a change of scenery. They returned to Croglin Grange the next spring. Shortly after their arrival, the mysterious being again entered the woman's room. One of the brothers chased the creature and shot it in the leg, but he was unable to stop it from entering the church graveyard. Terrified, the brothers waited for daybreak, then traced the monster's path to a burial vault. All but one of the corpses inside the vault had been removed from their caskets. They unsealed the only remaining undisturbed casket and found a body with a bullet wound in one of its legs. Fearing the corpse was indeed the vampire that had attacked their sister, the brothers removed the body and burned it.

THE HIGHGATE VAMPIRE

The case of the Highgate Vampire is an intriguing account of modern vampire activity. In 1967, Elizabeth Wojdyla and her friend claimed to have seen vampires rising from graves as they walked past the Cemetery of St. James in a section of London called Highgate. Wojdyla began to have nightmares about a ghoulish figure trying to enter her bedroom. The nightmares subsided, only to return two years later. Around that time she began showing mysteri-

In 1967 Elizabeth Wojdyla (left) claimed to have seen vampires in London's Cemetery of St. James (below).

Vampire expert Sean Manchester enters a vault at the Cemetery of St. James (below).

After allegedly discovering a vampire inside the vault, Manchester sealed it with a garlic-cement mix.

ous signs of a vampire attack. She was extremely weak and had two puncture marks on her neck. Vampire expert Sean Manchester was asked to investigate the case. He placed garlic, crosses, and holy water in her room. The visitations stopped, and her condition improved.

In 1970, a second woman reported having nightmares about a vampire visiting her in her sleep. Manchester was again called to investigate. While sleepwalking, the woman led Manchester to an aboveground crypt at the Cemetery of St. James. Inside the crypt, Manchester found three empty coffins. He lined them with garlic, placed a cross in each one, and sprinkled them with holy water.

Do Vampires Exist?

This woman led Sean Manchester to an aboveground crypt (pictured) in the Cemetery of St. James in 1970.

Later that year, Manchester entered another vault and found what he thought was the body of a real vampire. He read an **exorcism** to drive out the evil spirit, then sealed the vault with a garlic-cement mixture.

In 1977, Manchester returned to Highgate to investigate yet another vampire case. He found a coffin hidden inside a mansion basement near the cemetery. When he opened it, he was terrified but amazed. Staring back at him was the same vampire corpse he had exorcised seven years earlier. This time he drove a stake through the body, pinning it to the ground, and burned the body and the coffin.

Many vampire believers point to the Highgate Vampire case as proof these monsters walk among the living. Others say it was just an elaborate hoax and that vampires exist only in the minds of those who want to believe they are real. While this fascinating case may never be settled, others have been.

 Chapter 3

Vampires and Science

Accounts of vampire sightings are often very mysterious, but not entirely unbelievable. There usually seems to be a small amount of truth in some of these stories, even if many of the events described seem so unreal. This has led some scientists and other researchers to study vampires and the many stories about them. These studies may help explain the centuries-old belief in vampires.

One of the classic signs of a vampire, according to many stories, is the state of the body that has been unearthed from the grave. Many stories feature villagers digging up corpses of people suspected of being vampires. For example, in 1836 the body of a Serbian man thought to be a vampire, Milos Rakovic, was dug up

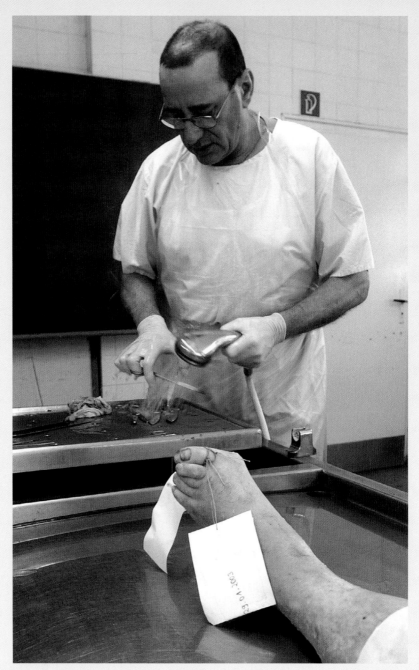

A scientist prepares to examine a corpse in a laboratory. The study of corpses has helped scientists explain many vampire mysteries.

three separate times. In this particular case, and in many others, the villagers were surprised by what they saw. The skin had not yet rotted away, but instead had a healthy reddish tint that seemed to suggest the body was still alive.

Additionally, the corpse of a suspected vampire often had blood streaming out of its nose and mouth. In the case of Arnold Paole, blood had soaked his burial clothes and coffin, as if he had consumed so much blood it was seeping out of his body. Finally, with many corpses that were dug up, old fingernails had fallen off and new ones appeared to have replaced them. For the vampire hunter, all of these horrifying signs seemed to confirm that the body was not dead, but undead.

Uncovering the Truth

Scientists today know that many of these mysterious signs of vampirism can be explained. They have learned that a corpse's rate of decay often depends on the body's temperature. For example, scientists who study corpses know that cool temperatures preserve a dead body longer than warm temperatures. Therefore, if the temperature of the soil surrounding a coffin is cool, the body inside may not **decompose**, or rot away, for several weeks. The corpse's reddish skin also is a natural part of the decomposition process. The coloration results from blood saturating the tissues beneath the skin.

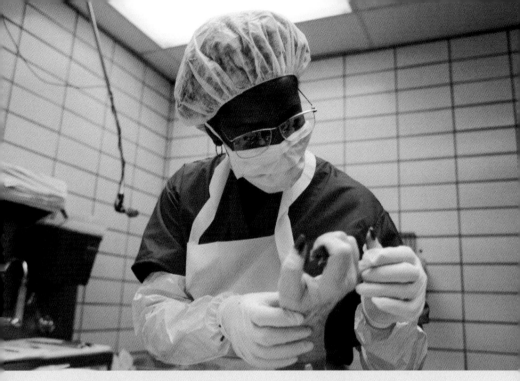

A medical examiner studies a corpse's fingernails, which can appear to be growing after death.

Blood, fingernail growth, and even the sound of escaping air may not necessarily be evidence of vampirism, either. A corpse naturally bloats due to gases being released within the body. This forces blood out of the nose, the mouth, and even the ears. And what might look like new fingernails might actually be layers of fresh-looking skin beneath old nails that have fallen off. Even the groan the military doctors reported hearing when they ran a stake through Paole's body can be explained. Air often remains inside a corpse's lungs well after death. When the corpse is moved–or in Paole's case, staked–the air passes between the vocal cords, causing a sound similar to the shout or cry of a living person.

 Vampires

BURIED ALIVE

For much of human history, people had no real knowledge of science or medicine. They often mistook one condition for another. For example, when a person falls into a trancelike state, the muscles stiffen and the heartbeat slows. In some cases, the person might appear to be dead. Today this condition is known as **catalepsy**.

The plague offers another example of medical misunderstanding. This terrible illness could so weaken the body that the sufferer might appear to be dead. The sick person's breathing and heart rate were almost nonexistent.

A person suffering from catalepsy or the plague long ago might have been buried alive. If that person

A man buried alive forces the lid from his coffin in this nineteenth-century illustration.

was later suspected of being a vampire, as happened sometimes, the corpse would have been dug up. It could have shown unusual characteristics. Accounts from centuries ago describe torn burial cloth, dried blood covering the lips, and a look of terror frozen on the person's face.

To the frightened peasant who uncovered the grave, this horrific image was proof the corpse was undead. But vampire researchers have offered another explanation. They believe the burial clothing was torn

A plague victim lies dead in this seventeenth-century painting. Some plague sufferers, weak with sickness, appeared dead and were buried alive.

when the person thrashed back and forth while trying to escape. The dried blood likely came from gnashing the teeth and accidentally biting the tongue. And the terrified look on the corpse's face was the result of a painful, suffocating death. Even Montague Summers, a firm believer in vampires, conceded that premature burial "may have helped to reinforce the tradition of the vampire and the phenomenon of vampirism."[7]

VAMPIRE DISEASES

Rare medical conditions have also been mistaken for signs of vampirism. For example, **furious rabies**, a severe form of rabies, causes night wanderings and body and facial contortions. Even the sight of a mirror and the smell of garlic can send a rabid person into a fit of rage. The disease leads to coma and ends in death.

With vaccines and medical treatments available today, the disease is rare. But historical documents show the disease reached epidemic proportions in Hungary during the early 1700s. This was also when vampire sightings were becoming more frequent in that part of Europe. Vampire experts believe dogs and wolves spread the disease to humans through biting. This may help to explain the rise of the vampire legend in Europe.

Porphyria, a rare blood disorder, is another medical condition that has been linked to vampirism. A person with this disease has abnormal **hemoglobin**, the part of the blood that assists in carrying oxygen through the body. The disease makes people extremely sensitive to light, causes extra hair to grow on the face and hands, and turns the teeth and eyes red. A person with this condition might look like a vampire to someone who does not know about the disease.

But sometimes even experts believe there is a connection between porphyria and vampirism. In 1985, a Canadian scientist named David Dolphin wrote an article tying the two conditions together. The usual treatment for this disorder today is injection of heme, a component of blood that helps oxygen bind to hemoglobin atoms. Such treatment was unknown centuries ago. Without heme, Dolphin believes, sufferers would have craved blood and tried to alleviate their symptoms by drinking it. The article caused a stir and the media began calling porphyria the vampire disease. Although scientists later learned there was no evidence the disease led to a desire to drink blood, Dolphin's image of bloodthirsty porphyria patients stuck. Today there are still people who believe this rare blood disorder is a reasonable explanation for vampires in the past.

Many of the old vampire superstitions have been disproved, yet this monster continues to stir the imagination and frighten the soul. This is because the vampire has made the transition from a monster that is possibly real to a phenomenon of popular culture.

CHAPTER 4

A Classic Monster

T oday vampires are everywhere. They are featured in novels and movies and on cereal boxes and stamps. This creature of the night truly has become an enduring part of modern popular culture. The steps it took to reach this level of popularity began more than 150 years ago. At that time, it made its first wide-scale appearance in literature.

The first vampire novel published in the English language was *Varney the Vampire, or the Feast of Blood* by James Malcom Rymer. The 1847 novel was not a huge success because it was long and difficult to read. But it managed to inspire a number of authors, particularly Bram Stoker, to write their own vampire tales.

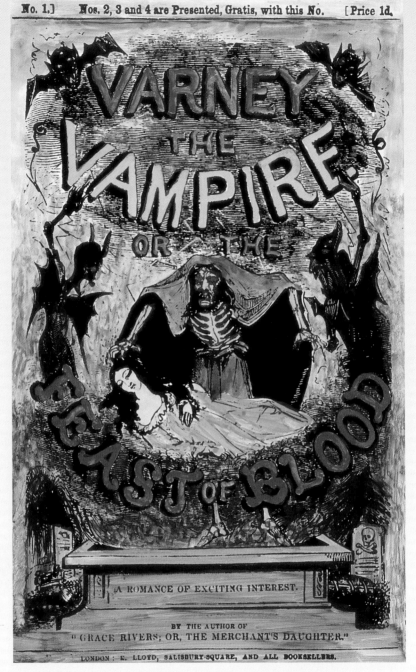

No. 1.]   Nos. 2, 3 and 4 are Presented, Gratis, with this No.   [Price 1d.

Published in 1847, Varney the Vampire *was the first English-language vampire novel.*

Bram Stoker based his 1897 novel Dracula *on a fifteenth-century prince named Vlad Dracula (pictured).*

Stoker loosely based his 1897 novel *Dracula* on a real person named Vlad Dracula, a fifteenth-century prince. For his novel, he also selected the vampire traits of old he thought were most frightening, such as the idea of the undead rising from the grave to drink the blood of others. He combined fact and fiction to create the evil Count Dracula. Stoker's vampire had pale skin, white hair, and a long, white mustache. He dressed in black and had hair on his palms. He also had pointed ears and foul-smelling breath. A dark and decaying stone castle in Transylvania was his home. The creepy setting and the count's bloodthirsty ways terrified readers and, according to author Matthew Bunson, "established forever the vampire as part of the popular folklore of the West."[8]

More than seventy-five years later, author Anne Rice gained a loyal following with her novel *Interview with a Vampire*. Rice's fictional vampire character, Lestat de Lioncourt, differed from Stoker's popular vampire. Lestat would not drink the blood of his innocent victims. Nor could he be harmed by religious objects or the sun. Rice kept the vampire in the spotlight by writing several other popular novels. They are part of a series known as the Vampire Chronicles, which remains highly popular today.

THE VAMPIRE TAKES HOLLYWOOD

The vampire's first real starring role on the big screen came in Universal's 1931 epic *Dracula*. The movie was based on Stoker's novel, but changes were made to Count Dracula's appearance. Gone were the grotesque physical features from the story. The "new" Dracula was played by a tall and handsome Hungarian actor named Bela Lugosi. The evil count dressed in formal wear and spoke in a foreign accent. But beneath Dracula's suave exterior was a terrifying figure. He had a ghostly white face, hypnotic eyes, and above all a thirst for blood. Lugosi's masterful performance and director Tod Browning's dramatic style so terrified audiences that some moviegoers passed out in their seats. Today, the black-and-white movie is considered one of the most influential horror movies of all time. It not only helped to define the category of horror movies but established the look of the modern vampire.

By today's movie standards, *Dracula* seems tame. When Lugosi moved in for the attack, the scene either slowly faded to black or cut to another scene. In the 1950s, though, the public saw a meaner, hungrier, and more terrifying count. Hammer Films' 1958 release of *Horror of Dracula* offered an updated version of the 1931 classic. British actor Christopher Lee donned Dracula's cape and was instantly accepted as the new face of evil. Unlike Lugosi, Lee wore long fangs and used them frequently. Instead of cutting away at the moment of attack, audiences saw Lee bite into his victim. The

Hungarian actor Bela Lugosi plays a bloodthirsty vampire in the 1931 film Dracula.

Blood drips from Dracula's fangs in this poster advertising the 1958 film Horror of Dracula.

movie's ending also added a new twist. Instead of dying from a stake through the heart, as had happened in the original movie, Lee's character died when he was exposed to sunlight.

The vampire continued to evolve on the big screen. In 1992, Francis Ford Coppola brought vampire fans *Bram Stoker's Dracula,* a movie that was closer to the nineteenth-century novel than the Lugosi and Lee versions had been. Dracula, played by actor Gary Oldman, regained the grotesque features made famous in Stoker's novel. He had hairy palms, foul breath, and pointed ears. The movie drew in a new generation of fans and made Count Dracula a vampire for the ages.

TELEVISION STAR

The vampire has long been portrayed in Hollywood films as a dark and bloodthirsty being. But this image changed briefly in the 1960s. Television viewers saw a harmless new vampire with the comedy show *The Addams Family.* The female vampire, Morticia Addams, was the mother who slept inside a coffin in a comical household of human and monster characters. *The Munsters,* a similar television comedy, featured two vampires named Lily and Grandpa Munster. The houseful of harmless monsters provided hilarious high jinks and some surprises. During the course of the show, viewers learned that Grandpa was actually a nearly four-hundred-year-old count from Transylvania. Though both series were short-lived, they continue

The vampire Count Von Count is a regular character on the children's television show Sesame Street.

to add new generations of fans through reruns. At times, vampires have even been tame enough for preschool children. *Sesame Street,* the long-running children's show, has featured a vampire puppet named Count von Count for many years.

In the 1990s, vampire shows offered a unique blend of drama and dark comedy. *Buffy the Vampire Slayer,* based on the 1992 movie, featured a teenage cheerleader who battled the undead. Played by

Sarah Michelle Gellar, Buffy used her athleticism and brains to defeat her vampire enemies. *Angel,* a spin-off from *Buffy the Vampire Slayer,* starred David Boreanaz as Angelus, a 240-year-old vampire who lost the desire to kill. Like Buffy, he too confronted bloodthirsty vampires on a weekly basis. Though neither show is currently still in production, they each have a devoted fan base that promises to keep vampires alive through fan clubs and Web sites.

Fangs for Everything

Through novels, movies, and television, vampires have reached popular culture stardom. The proof is in the countless toys, games, collectibles, and other

Actress Kristy Swanson drives a stake through a vampire's heart in the 1992 movie Buffy the Vampire Slayer.

items that now feature vampires. Sometimes the undead can show up in the strangest places, such as at the breakfast table. Count Chocula, the chocolate puffed cereal, features a cartoon vampire based on the classic Dracula character.

Vampires have also come in the mail. In 1997, the U.S. Postal Service introduced a stamp called *Bela Lugosi as Dracula*. The stamp showed Lugosi peering ominously over his tall collar. It was part of a series of stamps called the Classic Movie Monsters.

Other modern-day sightings include vampire video games such as the Buffy the Vampire Slayer series, *Vampires of Earth*, and *Blade II*. Where this classic monster is most popular, however, is Halloween night. On this night each year, thousands of people put on white makeup, insert plastic fangs, and don the black cape of Dracula to bring this monster of old back to life.

From ancient superstition to literary character to popular culture phenomenon, according to vampire expert J. Gordon Melton, "no other creature in the world of horror has caused more fear, more dread, yet more fascination than the vampire."[9]

NOTES

CHAPTER 1: THE VAMPIRE STRIKES!

1. Quoted in Peter Guttmacher, *Legendary Horror Films*. New York: MetroBooks, 1995, p. 27.
2. Montague Summers, *The Vampire in Europe: True Tales of the Undead*. New York: Gramercy, 1996, p. 157.
3. Montague Summers, *The Vampire*. New York: Dorset, 1991, p. 6.
4. Matthew Bunson, *The Vampire Encyclopedia*. New York: Crown, 1993, p. 189.
5. Bunson, *The Vampire Encyclopedia*, p. 28.
6. Quoted in John V.A. Fine Jr., "In Defense of Vampires," *East European Quarterly*, March 1987.

CHAPTER 3: VAMPIRES AND SCIENCE

7. Quoted in J. Gordon Melton, *The Vampire Book*. Farmington Hills, MI: Visible Ink, 1999, p. 242.

CHAPTER 4: A CLASSIC MONSTER

8. Bunson, *The Vampire Encyclopedia*, p. 73.
9. Melton, *The Vampire Book*, p. xxvii.

Glossary

catalepsy: A temporary, comalike condition.

decompose: To break down by chemical processes.

exorcism: A religious act that expels a demon or other evil entity.

furious rabies: A severe form of rabies that affects the central nervous system and usually leads to death.

hemoglobin: The part of the red blood cell that transports oxygen from the lungs to all parts of the body.

mythological: Relating to mythology or myths.

nocturnal: Active at night.

porphyria: An extremely rare blood disease that makes people sensitive to light.

shape-shift: To change from one physical body to another, such as from human to animal.

undead: Neither living nor dead; the state a vampire is in.

vampire hunter: A person who attempts to track down and destroy vampires.

vampirism: Actions relating to or belief in a vampire.

For Further Exploration

Books

Jim Pipe, *In the Footsteps of Dracula*. Brookfield, CT: Millbrook, 1995. Gives brief passages based on Bram Stoker's novel *Dracula,* and includes information about Stoker, Vlad Dracula, vampire bats, and more.

Bram Stoker, *Dracula*. New York: Dorling Kindersley, 1997. An abbreviated version of the legendary Bram Stoker novel, along with matching illustrations and sidebars.

Ian Thorne, *Dracula*. New York: Macmillan, 1977. Explores the 1931 classic movie *Dracula* and a host of other vampire movies.

Shannon R. Turlington, Cheryl Kimball, and Christel A. Shea, *The Everything Kids' Monsters Book*. Avon, MA: Adams Media, 2002. Readers learn the origins, habits, and strengths of legendary monsters such as bigfoot, the Loch Ness monster, vampires, zombies, and more.

43

WEB SITES

Buffy the Vampire Slayer (www.buffy.com). UPN-based Web site devoted to the popular television program. Includes photos, fan newsletter, and trivia about the series.

National Geographic's Creature Feature: Vampire Bats (www.nationalgeographic.com/kids/creature_feature/0110/vampirebats.html). Site features descriptions of the vampire bat, where the bat can be found worldwide, and fun bat facts.

NetPets (www.chirpingbird.com/netpets/html/features/oct/ghostly.html). Examines the connection between animals and monsters, including the vampire bat and Dracula, and wolves and werewolves.

Welcome to Dracula's Castle (www.draculas castle.com). This Web site contains many pictures of Vlad Dracula's two castles, and some historical information on the Romanian prince who became the basis for the novel *Dracula*.

INDEX

Picture Credits

ABOUT THE AUTHOR

Raymond H. Miller is the author of more than fifty nonfiction books for children. He has written on a range of topics from poisonous animals to presidential trivia. He enjoys playing sports and spending time outdoors with his wife and two daughters.